Thrive!

D1825287

"We are at that very point in time when a 400-year-old age is dying and another is struggling to be born—a shifting of culture, science, society, and institutions enormously greater than the world has ever experienced." *—Dee Ward Hock, founder of VISA*

Thrive!

How to Succeed
in the
Age of the Customer

Steve Towers
Mark McGregor

Meghan-Kiffer Press
Tampa, Florida, USA
www.mkpress.com
Innovation at the Intersection of Business and Technology

ISBN10: 0-929652-41-X
ISBN13: 978-0-929652-41-2

Published by Meghan-Kiffer Press
310 East Fern Street — Suite G
Tampa, FL 33604 USA

Company and product names mentioned herein are the trademarks or
registered trademarks of their respective owners.

Meghan-Kiffer books are available at special quantity discounts for
corporate education and training use. For more information write Special Sales, Meghan-Kiffer Press, Suite G, 310 East Fern Street, Tampa,
Florida 33604 or email sales@mkpress.com

Meghan-Kiffer Press
USA

Printed in the United States of America.   SAN 249-7980
MK Printing 10 9 8 7 6 5 4 3 2 1

Foreword

"No sensible decision can be made any longer without taking into account not only the world as it is, but the world as it will be." *—Isaac Asimov*

Although many in Western economies are in a state of denial, we are undergoing the greatest reorganization in the business world since the Industrial Revolution. If you somehow haven't noticed it yet, there is a loud and clear wake-up call in the air that can be heard everywhere. It's called *globalization*, and it's being brought to you by three billion new capitalists from China, India, and the former Soviet Union.

No matter what industry you are in, no matter how successful you are, it's time to get ready for the world as it will be—a world where your customers have new choices from a sea of suppliers from across the globe.

You can no longer be just a seller to your customers, you now must bond with your customers so fully that you and your customers become one. In this eye-opening book, Towers and McGregor guide you in how to make your customers your greatest business asset. And that's exactly what you will need to do to thrive in the age of the fully empowered customer.

Peter Fingar

Executive Partner, Greystone Group
Author of *Extreme Competition: Innovation and the Great 21st Century Business Reformation*

Contents

"We can't solve problems by using the same kind of thinking we used when we created them."
—Albert Einstein

1. It's So Big You Can't See It

There have been times when the world has undergone change so great that it has been invisible to those people most affected. Consider the following:

- A farm laborer watches the arrival of a machine that can do the work of ten men; by a meager fire that night he discusses with his wife the prospect of moving closer to the nearest town to look for work.

- Two neighbors discuss how washday hasn't been the same since the black smoke started to pour from the factory chimney nearby; the factory has brought employment but all that burning must be the devil's work – it can't last long.

- An office worker welcomes the arrival of something called a PC; it will only have limited use but at least there will be more time to get some real work done.

Hindsight is a fine thing. Were these changes so difficult to see at the time? The mechanization of agriculture; the Industrial Revolution; the IT revolution; all were dramatic changes that began slowly and developed in a way that few could predict. But there were a few who saw the changes coming, and now we can look back at the foresight of mill owners, industrialists and technology visionaries and marvel. Wouldn't it have been great to live in those times knowing what we know now? To have had the opportunity to be in at the beginning of something big? Well everything works in cycles and there is another cycle beginning right now. The big difference is that everybody can play their part and see the benefits. It's an opportunity that is not limited to those with money or power or to those who have already made their move. You can make a difference, right now.

What is needed above all is a change of attitudes. There is one common factor to the great changes that have taken place over the history of commerce – they have been about how work is done. It is about time that much more consideration is given to why businesses exist and who for. As will become clear as you read this book, we believe that a correction is long overdue in the priorities that organizations have.

There have never been more words about customers and their importance and yet so much discontent with the services and products offered. There may be many explanations for this apparent conundrum. The most likely is that people have become more demanding, and businesses have responded by talking a lot about how important their customers are. In many cases though, actions have not matched the words. Our aim here is to address this lack of action by shifting perceptions and changing mindsets at all levels. There are always rewards available for the people who start to make a difference in their organization, particularly when the result is happier customers and healthier profits.

You may have noticed that the language of business is often about the battle between companies and customers. Have you ever thought that there is something odd about this divide? Is our society segregated into customers and workers, two separate groups struggling for supremacy? Of course not. The people who make businesses work are customers themselves. Somewhere along the line many companies seem to have forgotten this. If your organization was run by its customers would it run differently? Very differently? And don't think that this is a mantra for giving everything away for nothing in pursuit of sales. Keeping customers happy and having a successful business should not be a battle of competing priorities. It's about time more companies realized that this internal battle is slowly (and in some cases not so slowly) killing them.

We will talk about how organizations must bring a radically different perspective to bear on the way they do business. There is a section of the book that covers this in much more detail, but until you get there, think about this: what aspect of you as a customer could you bring to your job that you don't already?

You will have your own examples of the great and the ugly in the world of customer service (and we'd love to hear them, by the way). For this book we have picked situations that are relevant and real. They have happened to us, to people we know, or to people who have cared enough about their experiences to tell us about them. We will tell some of these stories through the experiences of Thomas Everyman, a fictional character who represents normal, everyday people trying to make some sense of the situations they find themselves in.

Hopefully you will identify with some of what happens to Tom. By the way, don't fall into the failure trap of believing that your circumstances are out of the ordinary, that your situation is a special case. If you are reading this, you must have an interest in how to make things better. If you don't think any of this applies to you then congratulations, you are working in an organization that is so great it can't improve any further. (It might be worth spending a few moments to rethink, before you move on).

While it hopefully makes for easier reading than many books of its type, using Tom Everyman's experiences will also emphasize the importance of individuals in all of this. As individuals we can all take some control over the changes that will be taking place in the months and years to come and reap the rewards. In any great changes in society there have always been winners and losers. Many new jobs have been created with better pay and working conditions, while the need for new skills has excluded others. New businesses have been born and prospered, while others have gone to the wall despite their size and history. The wealth of many has increased, sometimes unimaginably, but with that has come the stress to deliver ever greater value and work ever longer hours. Everybody should want to play their own part in making sure that they are on the winning side.

We are not about to wave a magic wand that will make all of the bad stuff go away. A new approach does raise the prospect of generating profitable business from happier customers through the activities of motivated employees. It doesn't have to be as bad as it is in many organizations, where the only common ground between staff and customers seems to be discontent with the current state of affairs. So this isn't a detailed textbook on how to change the world in so many easy steps. Neither is it theoretical waffle. The emphasis is on changing bad attitudes and strengthening good ones, with some practical help to get you on your way. After decades of neglect and being taken for granted, it's time for the customer in each of us to strike back, from within and without.

"Simplicity is the ultimate sophistication."
—Leonardo da Vinci

2. How Did It Get This Bad?

John Maynard Keynes (English economist, journalist and financier) once said "The difficulty lies, not in the new ideas, but in escaping the old ones." This quote may be decades old but it has real resonance today. Outdated mindsets are the biggest obstacles to an organization's ability to realign itself to new priorities. To really understand why most of us work in the way that we do today, it's important to look back at how things have evolved. This isn't a history book so you're not going to get a detailed review of the development of organized work in the world. We will concentrate on the key periods.

First there was the Agrarian Age, where farming was based on individual labor. Many people worked on the land in what was a slowly evolving version of the way people had been living for many centuries. The Industrial Age followed, with mechanization and large-scale organization taking over. Factories came to the fore, and people found themselves corralled like the livestock they had once tended. Mass production came to be the dominant method of manufacturing; machinery replaced people in the execution of repetitive activities. More recently, we have seen the Information Age emerge quickly, with exponential growth in computing power, data storage and communications technologies driving immense changes in our business capabilities.

The changes brought about during these periods have been dramatic. The landscapes and skylines that surround us bear the scars and silhouettes of our evolving workplace: vast fields that make industrial farming possible; redundant cotton mills and canal-side warehouses converted into office blocks. Western economies that have embraced these changes to the greatest extent have benefited from rapid growth in standards of living, and now other parts of the world are experiencing these changes for themselves. As well as being periods of great change these Ages of Work, as we will call them, have one other aspect in common: they have focused on how work has been done. New capabilities as much as anything have brought the new Ages of Work into being: the steam engine; iron smelting; the production line; the PC; the Internet. There are many others. It is not surprising that there is a persistent emphasis in business on *how*: how to organize, how to reduce cost, how to make more. Company restructuring is probably the most visible aspect of this obsession.

You may be familiar with this quote:

> "We trained hard ... but it seemed that every time we were beginning to form up into teams we would be reorganized. I was to learn later in life that we tend to meet any new situation by reorganizing; and a wonderful method it can be for creating the illusion of progress while producing confusion, inefficiency, and demoralization."

The quote is often attributed to Petronius, a courtier of the Roman emperor Nero, but it is probably a much more recent jibe at authority by a disillusioned WWII soldier. Nevertheless it very eloquently describes most people's experience of company reorganization. The place that many organizations start when addressing a new challenge is their internal structure. The problem is that most organizations don't know enough about what they are trying to achieve before they embark on changing how they operate.

The hierarchy is the dominant form of management structure today. Companies, public institutions, voluntary groups all cling to the rigid hierarchies that were needed to make Industrial Age production operations work. The structure evolved to meet the challenge of organizing large numbers of people carrying out set tasks and has been very successful in allowing great steps forward in productivity (and winning a few wars). The "management pyramid" underpins many of today's working practices, our understanding of how to make labor efficient, and most theories about leadership.

Not only has the hierarchy survived, but the division of activities into functions also persists. If there was a "bring your great-grandparents to work" day where you work, how much would be familiar to them from their working days? Okay, so the computer equipment, air conditioning and lack of smoking would be new. How long would it take to explain that there's a sales team, an accounts team, people

looking after operations and so on? About two minutes in most cases. Show them a structure chart and
they will tell you who the top man is (oh yes, there
probably aren't that many more women in those jobs
than there were in great-granddad's day, but that's
another story). In fact the functional split is so deep-
seated that whole careers are now spent in one function. Narrow specialisms have developed in the largest companies (organization design, management information and the like), which have become self-
perpetuating, further focusing attention internally.
The more entrenched these divisions, the more difficult the job becomes of joining everything together
well.

It's no accident that the tools commonly used to
draw organization charts default (if indeed there are
any other options) to an arrangement of boxes joined
by straight lines, with "bigger jobs" towards the top
and team members arranged in lines beneath. If these
applications defaulted to a series of concentric circles
with the customer in the middle, might some organizations end up looking a little different? Where would
the "big jobs" be? Would functions dominate the division of responsibilities or might customer-facing
activities have more sway?

Structures should exist to help make things happen, so it should be pretty clear from the outset what
these important things are. There are companies that
set strict guidelines for how many hierarchical levels
should exist and how wide spans of control should
be. We know of companies where the latter constraint

is driven by the demands of performance management on team leaders. If a company's performance management systems have a big influence on team structures then the performance management systems need fixing.

Measuring the success of a business has to be more than just looking at the bottom line. Companies have to broaden their outlook and look beyond short term financial indicators. An important measure of a company's success must be its ability to improve performance continuously. Truly successful companies understand and actively manage what influences their people to do the right things every day. And the important phrase here is "do the right things." As we have already said, if performance targets are linked to corporate objectives that aren't customer-focused then more and more dumb stuff gets done. But most objectives are inward-looking and often functionally specific. Consequently, most staff reward mechanisms are based on the traditional production mindset of doing more things, working more quickly, fitting in well, and playing the game.

Put another way, rewards are linked to "doing something to something to get something." Where objectives are truly focused on the customer, and people have the flexibility to do the right things, there is less need to impose so much structure on people. Organization structures then become *support* mechanisms rather than *control* mechanisms.

In summary, our heritage of working methods explains a lot about the way we work today. Hierarchies evolved to meet the challenge of organizing large numbers of people carrying out set tasks. They have served us well but the world is moving on.

The challenge for organizations is to be more agile, flexible, and responsive to changing customer needs. Companies across the world have indulged in restructuring that has focused on moving chairs around, while avoiding the key issue: that the structures they are trying to apply aren't fit for purpose in the new world. And this new world isn't limited to big business and its customers: the provision of public services to citizens, all business to business activity, in fact every relationship between people and organizations is in need of an overhaul.

The need to reassess and fundamentally realign structures and priorities is paramount. Any organization that can't make the leap must face the prospect of being left behind in this new age – the Age of the Customer.

"Reality is the cage of those who lack imagination."
— J. B. S. Haldane

3. So What's the Answer?

The opportunities for organizations to reach a level of customer orientation that will transform them are enormous. Sadly history and experience show that opportunities are often seen as challenges and obstacles, to be worried about, avoided, and perhaps ignored completely. The principal purpose of this book is to convey the message that customer expectations are changing, and changing rapidly. To survive, the organizations that interact with them (us!) need to grasp what is going on and respond.

Expectations have changed as we have become better educated and informed about the buying decisions we make. We want the organizations that we do business to with to show that they understand what we need and can deliver it. Preferably they will spot what we want before we do! This demands flexibility and agility from the businesses that want to gain and keep *satisfied* customers. At the same time competition is growing: this era of globalization is seeing vibrant new economies emerging. Not only are the Asian economies taking away the drudge and administration from many businesses, they are also doing that work better. Let's look at how any organization can set itself on the way to being really customer-oriented.

Do you spend a long time waiting for elevators to arrive? This is a common problem in large buildings with many people – busy elevators have to stop at all floors, slowing their progress and increasing the frustration of those waiting for one to arrive. The answer has often been to put in more elevators, but this causes problems elsewhere, notably in the reduction of valuable office space. Some manufacturers and developers have looked to smaller, quicker elevators to alleviate the problem but have come up against capacity issues.

Otis Elevators took a different view and looked at the way the Japanese railway system works. In Japan, as in many countries, there are both local and express rail services. The difference is that they run on separate tracks meaning that the slow trains do not hold up the express services. When you arrive at the station the train you need is determined by your destination, the time you want to take, and how much you want to pay. Otis took that idea and came up with a control panel in the elevator lobby – you put in your security card (the mechanism doubles as an ID system), key in the floor that you want to go to, and it tells you which lift will get you there the quickest. They have been able to reduce the number of lifts, increase capacity, and improve the experience. Otis now leads the elevator market.

What Otis Elevators have done is a great example of innovation based on Successful Customer Outcomes (SCOs). To achieve this leap forward in the market they have done three things:

- Understood who their real customers are;
- Worked out what was needed to satisfy these cus-

tomers (the SCOs);
- Made sure that they can deliver effectively against these SCOs.

We can use these three straightforward steps as the basis for an action plan, a plan that can help any organization to place the customer at the center of its activities. As we have already said this emphasis isn't just in the words that the organization uses but in everything that the company does, from the way that it structures itself, through performance rewards, to innovation. Being a business driven by SCOs also means moving away from the constraints of Industrial Age thinking – big hierarchies, functional stovepipes and limiting improvement to the best practice seen in competitors (more on this in Chapter 7). We will look at each of these steps in turn:

1. Work out the customers whose needs you are trying to meet, and understand those needs well

A fundamental requirement for defining good SCOs is to make sure you are concentrating on the right "C." You will have heard the phrase "the customer is always right." Well that's not true, at least not in the way that it is often used: "*every* customer is always right!"

Some companies are so knotted up with pleasing everybody that they are unable to fully service the needs of the customers that are most important to them. There are always customers who don't fit well with what a company is trying to do, so be prepared to lose them, so that you can better focus on the customers that you do want. If that sounds like heresy, then think in terms of *custom* rather than customer – there are certain needs that you can't or don't want to meet. It's not the individual that you are dismissing.

It's also important to differentiate between core customers and enabling customers. Otis Elevators has been successful by focusing on the true customer (the elevator user) but without losing sight of the people that buy the equipment they build, the developers and employers. The spark of differentiation comes from delivering to the real end-user; the rest is about getting the delivery right.

So, knowing your customers' needs is a vital part of the process of delivering distinctive offerings. Too many organizations suffer from what we call Customer Attention Deficit Disorder – the inability to focus consistently on customers and their needs. Getting this right needs more than an occasional visit to the frontline or the shop floor. Henry Ford knew what he was talking about when he said, "if I had asked what they wanted, they would have said faster horses." It requires a deep-seated understanding of what is needed throughout the business, not just the results of last week's telephone survey.

Once you are clear on the customers that you want to serve and what their needs are, the next step is converting that knowledge into clear objectives:

2. Keep everything clear and simple and focused on the customer

Consider these two quotations:

"Everything should be made as simple as possible, but not simpler."

"Simplicity is the ultimate sophistication."

These are not the words of slackers. They come from two of the greatest brains in human history, Albert Einstein and Leonardo da Vinci, respectively. These two guys could deal with whatever level of complexity confronted them, so this desire for the right level of simplicity had nothing to do with their intellectual ability. If only that were true of many organizations. How often do we see complexity within organizations, in structure, product range or literature, which is worn almost as a badge of distinction? Every company needs a clear, concise statement of what it exists to do in terms of Successful Customer Outcomes. SCOs are about bringing the reality in line with the vision, so they must be simple. The more involved they are, the more difficult they are to understand and deliver.

Here's an example of what happens when what should have been a simple need for customers to be able to reach their destination easily and quickly becomes lost in the quest for solutions.

Tom Everyman waited patiently for the guy behind the counter at the car airport rental booth to complete the paperwork and let him have the key.

"Do you have any maps of the area, please?" he asked. "I'm not sure how to get to my hotel."

With a beam of satisfaction the clerk looked up from the triplicate forms he was filling in. "No need for that, sir. We have our new navigation aid in all of our cars now."

Tom had heard that at least one of the car rental firms had put satellite navigation in their fleet. He hadn't expected it at the budget end of the market his company travel policy demanded.

Soon furnished with key and documents, Tom made his way to the car, looking forward to a stress free drive and a long bath at the hotel. After several frustrating minutes of trying to find the navigation system, Tom consulted the manual in the glove box. The only reference he could find was to the cell phone in the cradle on the dash. He called the number in the manual.

"Good evening, Hire-A-Car navigation service, how can I direct you today?" said a friendly voice.

"It's a little embarrassing but I'm looking for the satellite navigation service in my rental car. It's a-"

"We operate a cell phone service, sir. Just tell me where you are and where you are going."

"You're going to give me … directions?" Tom's stress levels were rising already, the prospect of the soothing tones of in-car navigation now a distant dream. Tom tucked the "navigation aid" between his ear and shoulder and rooted for a pen and paper. The hotel suddenly felt a long way away.

A crisis is a good test of how customer-focused an organization is. British Airways struggled with industrial action during the Summer of 2005: staff from one of the airline's caterers went on strike over the sacking of colleagues and other airport workers came out in support. Amid all the strife an interview with the BA chief stood out. He laid out, in so many words, the priorities that were driving quick resolution of the dispute:

1. Profit
2. Pilots
3. Cabin crew
4. PR
5. Agents
6. Staff
7. Customers

It seemed pretty clear that customer considerations weren't leading the decision-making as the crisis unfolded. Although BA wasn't itself the cause of the dispute (the catering had been outsourced some time before) it had responsibilities: the customers affected were BA's. This is a lesson for all companies outsourcing some of their activities. Feeding passengers should have featured in BA's SCOs, and so it should have been in control of the processes that delivered that SCO. Whatever the chain of events that led to the disruption, BA was culpable because it did not let go of the customer relationship when it outsourced this activity. It seems to us that so much of BA's efforts are internally focused – giving more lines in the in-flight magazine to telling us how much has been spent on lounge upgrades than telling us about how much better the experience will be. It is time for BA and many other such companies to start thinking from the outside in.

3. Align the organization to the SCOs

Processes are the delivery mechanisms for SCOs, so getting the processes right is a vital part of the alignment activity. Many companies are looking at their processes and developing process dictionaries and the like, but if this isn't done within the context of SCOs then there is the great risk of just doing the wrong thing more efficiently. There are many techniques available to review and refine processes (more of this in Chapter 6) – what should emerge though isn't a set of projects but an ongoing mechanism for ensuring that the company "machinery" is delivering the SCOs.

In Chapter 2 we talked about the lingering impact of reorganization on company effectiveness. Changing a structure without understanding customer needs and how they are to be delivered simply produces a new way of getting things wrong. The inertia created by functional structures and specialisms should not be underestimated. Layers of hierarchy also serve to place leaders a long way from where the customer interaction is. Companies built around SCOs don't look like this. They can be, and are, flatter.

Take Morning Star for instance. In a case study on the world's leading tomato processor, based in California, Doug Kirkpatrick describes how Morning Star operates without hierarchy – the organization is literally as flat as one of the pizza bases its products are often found in contact with. The only boss is the mission statement, and the guiding principle is self-management. There aren't even any job titles. Feeling uncomfortable yet? Or liberated?

There's no doubt that this is a working environment for those who can cope with not being told what to do (and who don't need to have people around to order about either). But that's what you would want, isn't it? What is fascinating is that leadership is as important, if not more so, in the flat organization: everyone has to be a leader.

Doug writes tellingly about the benefits of running a business like this:

> "Morning Star has found that organizational energy can be tapped and orchestrated (not manipulated) by tapping into the self-interest and motivation of individual colleagues, identifying an issue around which they have a stake, identifying a leader who has the expertise to deal with the issue, and giving people the choice of following and contributing."

Many organizations aspire to achieve this, but how many are committed enough to sweep away the hierarchy that's getting in the way? Not only does Morning Star run with no management pyramid, they focus completely on the activities that deliver value to their customers. The contrast between the state of the art production facilities and simple administrative systems says everything about the priorities of the business. First and foremost the company is about delivering Successful Customer Outcomes – everything else is organized in support of this.

One way of looking at the relationship between a business and its customer base is as a solar system, where the customers act like the sun, influencing how the other parts work together. If our solar system functioned like most companies then planets would revolve around each other with the sun looking on bewildered. So rather than trying to decide which of your organization's planets (or functions) everything should revolve around, get it fixed in your mind that the energy-giving customer is at the center of everything and allow the rest to follow from that.

Planets have it easy in one way – they have no option but to submit to the natural forces, such as gravity, that determine their orbits. Organizations however can choose to what extent they allow market forces to dictate how they operate. The best companies use these forces to propel them forwards, and they do this by getting their people aligned with what they are trying to achieve.

Where objectives are truly focused on Successful Customer Outcomes and people have the flexibility to do the right things, there is less need to impose so much structure on people. Organization structures then become support mechanisms rather than control mechanisms.

The need for organizations to be agile and flexible while aligning to customer needs is illustrated in the following diagram:

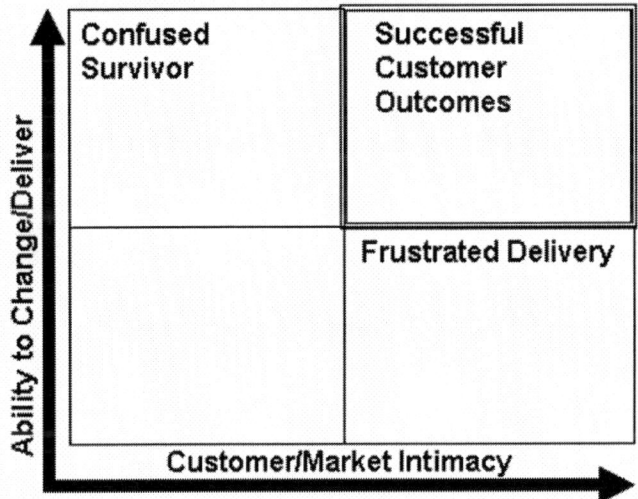

Figure 1. SCOs require both internal and external capabilities

The ability of an organization to change is largely a function of the degree to which it is process-driven, so process management is a clear enabler toward realizing SCOs. Process management also helps organizations to take a customer perspective and work out what changes are required.

The challenge is clear, and we have only touched on some of the questions facing organizations intent on transforming themselves. There is one question that we hear more than any other, although it's not often asked directly: How quickly does my organization need to change? Of course there are many answers to this question, answers dictated by market, competition and many other factors. We will answer this question by briefly highlighting a great example of wholesale transformation to SCOs.

BT (formerly British Telecom) has moved from a cumbersome, inwardly focused hierarchical model to a much more agile, output-based structure in less than three years. It is now a market leader in this level of service orientation. If the largest organizations have already turned themselves outside-in, then the companies yet to start will need more than an express elevator if they are going to survive in the Age of the Customer.

So what should be done with the all of this learning? Well here's a tip – don't start from what you do now and look for incremental improvement. Companies with a short-term and predominantly cost reduction outlook pursue a periodic crash-diet approach to keeping themselves on target.

What's needed is a completely different approach – a healthy eating regime if you like, a permanent shift in habits and behaviors to get on the path to long term survival.

The gulf between the organizations that understand what SCOs are and structure themselves around them, and those that carry on with the same-old, same-old, is widening as we speak – in fact it's becoming a chasm.

So if you're not working out how to get across that chasm now, you are going to be one of those organizations that gets left behind, perhaps permanently. It just isn't good enough to get a bit better at what you are doing, the changes needed are fundamental. It's a new era, and that means new answers.

Case Study: Airlines Reach a New Service Altitude

We have looked at the concept of Successful Customer Outcomes – what we should seek out on behalf of our customers to ensure we meet and exceed their expectations. If we align our organizations to SCOs (rather than the silos of the Industrial Age) they become slicker, more agile, and indeed more profitable. The focus here is on travel, where some of the best companies are pulling away from the competition but are not yet doing as much as they can.

We'll start with sickness bags! This may not sound like a promising place to begin, but bear with us for a while. easyJet, a European budget airline, continues to grow at the expense of many of its rivals. These include the large international monoliths who have until recently operated with some impunity towards passenger comfort and fares. In an environment of rising fuel costs, terrorist threats, increasing competition and inflexible organization structures, it is bottom line cost performance that has become critical. This is even more pertinent for the budget carriers, where inexpensive items represent a large proportion of the ticket price. Many airlines have haphazardly reduced their offering to reduce the cost; easyJet has looked to innovate.

Taking an idea from Southwest Airlines, who advertise job vacancies on their sick bags, easyJet has gone that step further and removed the cost of the sickness bags by getting someone else to pay for them. Kodak provides the bags, which if unused (yuck!) can be employed as film envelopes for those vacation pictures. Even in this digital age many folks are wedded to their 35mm cameras. For the digitally liberated, Kodak also provides fast turnaround development services for photo media – you guessed it, right there in the arrivals lounge. easyJet of course can focus clearly on this type of opportunity because their Successful Customer Outcome, as articulated by their creator, Stelios, is "Buttocks on Seats."

So what SCO-inspired survival tips can we propose that may help the troubled airline giants to survive, if it isn't already too late? Let's see what some customers think.

The Joy of Flying

Tom Everyman collapsed into the seat in the departures lounge of Anytown airport. His friends Dick and Harry appeared to be in a similar state of nervous exhaustion, having finally negotiated the assault course known as check-in.

"I sometimes wish you could send the kids on ahead," he said to anyone listening. "You know, a large scale chaperone service. It would be so much easier – the airlines could clean up!"

Dick, who'd managed to get them all coffees, had different ideas. "I think there are a few more basic things they could do with getting right first."

"Go on then," said Tom, "we're all ears – anything to kill time until boarding." He reflected on why there had to be such a long time between arrival and getting on the plane. Perhaps that was one of the things Dick had in mind.

"Okay, take the kids," continued Dick. "You said you'd like to send them on ahead, but let's assume we're stuck with them."

"We might actually want to travel with them!" interrupted Harry.

"You always were the softy, Harry," said Tom.

"Anyway how about keeping them entertained?" Dick was pressing on. "Half of our hand luggage is taken up with stuff for the kids. I'd like more help with giving the kids something to do."

Harry was dismissive. "There are a few music channels, the in-flight movie. What more do you want?"

Dick was on a roll now. "What, those screens that hang over the seats? You should have been behind some of the heads and hairstyles that I've endured. Seat-back video is the only way. I've heard that some of the airlines are actually thinking about taking *out* screens to save weight and money. Next they'll be making us stand all the way!"

Tom was warming to Dick's ideas and found he had a suggestion of his own. "They could give us some way of plugging in all the stuff the kids have got – the games, mp3 players and the like. If I have to suffer another attack of battery rage …"

"Yes, but why do we have to bring all of our own stuff into the cabin?" Dick continued. "These things are all digital now – why not have a big library on board? It doesn't weigh anything."

"Except for the server, the cabling, the screens …" Harry, the IT expert, could always be relied on to plug the gaps in his friend's knowledge.

"Okay, okay, but that lot doesn't weigh as much as a couple of hundred Playstations and iPods, does it?"

"What about TV on-demand then, choosing which programs to watch? I might be able to keep an eye on what they're watching for once." Tom could barely contain his ideas now.

Dick brought him back to earth. "Sounds like you need parenting lessons, not in-flight entertainment."

What these guys are talking about would make traveling more than just a necessary burden: it would become part of the vacation itself. This is the market that airlines are in. Of course price is of critical importance, but not at the expense of everything else. Doing these things doesn't necessarily mean radical change; it just means doing the current things better, more imaginatively.

The technology is not expensive so what stops the others following suit? It's simple: focusing on the wrong things, having the wrong priorities, and clinging to the delusion that the current problems are just a temporary blip. In the same vein, here are two more ideas.

Reading is such a popular pastime on flights that a whole genre of fiction has developed – the airport novel. Easily read and soon forgotten these books tend not to find a permanent place on the bookshelf at home. Why not bring these books on board? Rather than buy them, customers could browse, read, and leave behind whatever took their fancy. Condensed novels, chapter samplers and short stories could also come into their own as word length and flight time are aligned. Book retailing is a competitive business, so there is a commercial angle that could be exploited. Intelligent use of sponsorship, discounts for subsequent purchases and other promotions should make this at least a cost-neutral offering. Perhaps the airlines are just waiting to exploit the technology that already exists to make e-books available. Should they get the benefit of the doubt?

What springs to mind when you think of in-flight coffee? The smell of fresh ground beans wafting along the aisle? Perhaps not. The coffee may taste so bad because it discourages us from asking for it, keeping the aisles clear for the more profitable activities like the duty free trolley. Sponsored coffee provision from the likes of Costa Coffee or Starbucks would raise the quality and cut the cost.

Of course it's not only the leisure traveler that airlines cater to. Business travel is big business, not that you would know it sometimes. While it can sometimes be a blessing for frequent fliers to get away from an always-on world, this should be a choice not an imposition. Most carriers take the imposition route and resist the straightforward step of services like in-flight Internet. Lufthansa did it in 2003 and offers full access to mail and the Web. That makes them the airline of choice for many who have little else to do as they traverse the skies of Europe. Some airlines insist that it's a large cost overhead and that regulation is an obstacle. Hogwash! With Teutonic efficiency the Germans are leading the way and will continue to win business as others procrastinate.

And don't try complaining about it by phone on the flight. Even the FAA isn't in the way of conversations at 35,000ft – they just carry the blame (quite wrongly) as airlines seek to protect their investments in hardwired back of the seat lumps of plastic that no one uses because of the expense. There are other areas ripe for improvement:

Fly Me to the Moon

There were still thirty minutes to boarding and Tom's mind was still on making the flying experience a bit more rewarding. "Harry, how many miles do you fly for work? Must be quite a number."

Harry answered quickly enough to give away that he knew the answer without having to work it out. "150,000 in the last year."

"Wow, and you've been doing that for years," said Dick. "That's astronaut-like mileage. You must have some views on business flying. Is there anything you'd fix?"

Harry thought ... for half a second. "Loads." Tom and Dick exchanged glances – the risk of spending the entire flight listening to Harry's litany of suggestions was great.

"What's your number one?" asked Tom.

"Easy," said Harry. "Frequent fliers. I don't see why those of us who fly regularly should be treated as non-paying passengers rather than loyal customers when we use the points we've earned. What's the point of only having access to off-peak flights for instance? I can understand the need to make individual flights profitable, but I'd say that inconveniencing your best customers is a strange way to run a successful business."

Tom had to agree, but could feel that Harry was working up a head of steam. He was right.

"You see, with a bit of imagination, frequent flier rewards could be used in-flight too: drinks, food upgrades, gifts. I don't mind being a walking advert for a loyalty program if I feel I'm getting the value I want. There's no harm in having other passengers asking 'how do I get those benefits, is there?'"

Dick started to answer the question. "Well, I…"

"And then there are upgrades," Harry wasn't to be stopped. "I tell you, for some airlines 'easy upgrade' is a contradiction in terms. I flew with a major national airline recently and discovered what's called a non-upgradeable ticket. I was bounced between check-in and what was laughingly called the Customer Service Desk to be told that I 'had bought the wrong ticket' and 'didn't understand how these things worked'! The attractive choices were to pay again for a completely new ticket or accept my fate. I chose the latter, and I can't tell you what I was thinking during that flight looking at those empty Business Class seats.

Harry, you're with the wrong airline," Dick said.

"A guy I know at work asked to upgrade recently using his loyalty miles, and they said 'that's okay sir,
we'll upgrade you without taking the miles!' Now
that's service."

Dick's story highlights one of the key points that
emerge from this look at airlines. Some of the most
striking experiences come from individuals being able
to do the right thing (even the unexpected thing)
when it matters. A Virgin flight attendant who apolo-
gizes for the fact that we are not flying on one of the
brand new aircraft in the fleet (but which is still is better than most); the generous and immediate compen-
sation for a mid-flight entertainment system failure.
These responses come from liberated staff in customer-focused organizations. Successful Customer
Outcomes come from, and are delivered through,
people – they should be given the opportunity to innovate to be great. What would their list of innova-
tions look like? Do you think they've been asked?

"There is only one boss, the customer. And he can fire everybody in the company from the chairman on down, simply by spending his money somewhere else."
—Sam Walton, founder of Wal-Mart

4. Giving Customer Service a "MoT"

Sam Walton expresses it so well: the customer is King. If we accept this reality, then we have to ask ourselves, how do we treat this VIP? It is a fundamental question and one that will have a profound effect on the way businesses operate for decades to come. It will also impact the very way in which we live our lives as individuals. The single biggest challenge for many of the people we see at courses and seminars is understanding how to treat their customers as royalty. They give the impression that, in most of their organizations, the majority of employees don't know who the customer is or how what they do supports the efforts of the organization to deliver on its promises. Yet, those same people are consumers too! And they are continually sharing their bad experiences in class. Some even laugh about their bad experiences as customers of their own companies.

Good customer experiences are what this is all about. Interestingly, if you search back into your own buying experiences you will find those good experiences. How did you feel? Good, right? So what are you doing now to create those experiences for your customers?

Thinking back to one of those great experiences, what made it good and what was different about it? Chances are that the experience occurred when something went wrong and somebody assisted you in a way that made things right again and made you feel good about it.

Making customers feel wanted is at the heart of implementing Successful Customer Outcomes. Any analysis of the factors that influence how any customer feels about an organization will show that it is that direct interaction that is crucial. This is where the concept of "Moments of Truth"' (MoT) comes in. MoT is a term coined by Jan Carlzon of Scandinavian SAS airlines and occurs every time that a customer interacts with an organization, whether indirectly (e.g., via the Internet) or with a person. Each of these MoTs will result in one of two outcomes. Either it will turn into a "Moment of Magic" where the customer goes away at least satisfied, but hopefully delighted. Or it becomes a "Moment of Madness," one of those occasions where the customer becomes extremely frustrated and possibly even angry.

It has to be the goal of any company to ensure that every MoT becomes a Moment of Magic, and there are a number of techniques that can be applied to ensure that these opportunities are optimized. As any good marketer will tell you, these happy customers are likely to tell three to five people how good you were. In the alternative scenario, those same marketers will tell you that those who experience Moments of Madness will tell as many as eight to ten people *not* to use you. In both cases the variance in numbers is proportional to how delighted or angry they were.

This view is supported by recent research by Marc Beaujean, Jonathan Davidson and Stacey Madge at McKinsey (*McKinsey Quarterly*: 2006 Number 1). Their work in retail banking showed that, after a Moment of Magic, over 85 percent of customers purchased more products or invested more of their assets, while more than 70 percent did the opposite after a Moment of Madness. The research also showed that the Moments of Truth that made most difference were those that happened when something went wrong. This highlights a challenging question for many organizations: is it worth investing heavily in the day-to-day interactions with customers when it is the correcting of problems after they happen that has the most positive impact? More on this later in the Chapter.

So ask yourself, how many Moments of Truth do you have each day with your customers? And how have you organized yourselves to ensure that each one of them becomes a Moment of Magic? And if you should cause a Moment of Madness to occur, how will you redress it to the customer's satisfaction?

We all know what it is to be a frustrated customer, and there must be a lot of them about if they have caused signage like this to appear:

> "Our people have the right to work in a safe and secure environment and we have a duty to protect those rights. Accordingly, anyone acting in an abusive manner, or us-

ing abusive language or physically assaulting
our staff will be prosecuted."

Before saying too much more on the subject we
should point out that any sort of intimidation, physi-
cal or otherwise, can never be tolerated and as such
deserves prosecution. But what are the causes of this
abuse that companies are referring to, and could it be
tackled in a different way?

As customers we pay for goods and services and
surely have a right to expect delivery. It seems today
that rather than focus on driving out the Moments of
Madness, businesses tell us we have no right to complain, or if we do it has to be quiet and we should accept a non-resolution to the problem! Generally this
consumer friction arises when the organization in
question has failed to deliver on a promise, turning
normally reasonable people into quivering wrecks.
Perhaps the obligation should be on the companies to
deliver on what they promise, thus eliminating the
cause of much of this behavior.

A very public example of the treatment that customers can receive at the hands of a "service" business is the experience of one Vincent Ferrari and his
attempts to cancel his father's AOL subscription. The
recording of the call made by Ferrari to AOL is extraordinary and has to be heard to be believed.[1]
As some commentators have pointed out, the appear-
ance and subsequent rapid spread of this story (and

---

[1] Listen at http://media.putfile.com/AOL-Cancellation

its audio evidence) demonstrates that bad customer service is no longer something that people have to suffer alone – it can be public property in a matter of minutes.

As we reflect on Moments of Truth we should start to see a number of things. First, they are person to person experiences (the guys we've already heard from at McKinsey talk about the "spark between the customer and frontline staff members—the spark that helps transform wary or skeptical people into strong and committed brand followers"). This means *people* are crucial when it comes to creating great customer experiences. Second, the fact that a person puts it right means enablers are needed to allow the person to engender those good feelings. *Process* is therefore critical to delighting customers and generating great experiences.

The third thing we can note, and we alluded to it earlier, is the fact that MoTs often occur after a bad experience. Many readers will see where this is going, in that we need to learn to think from the outside in. But just for a moment we can allow ourselves to look at things from the inside out, something that should be easy as we have spent most of the past 100 years thinking this way. So from the inside-out, how much time, money and resource do companies waste in generating the bad experience that triggers the good experience? How much waste does your organization generate in trying to deal with bad experiences and how much profit goes down the drain as a result?

Perhaps, like a hotel in South Africa we visited recently, you provide training courses for your staff in how to handle complaints and customer relation issues. When meeting with the management of the hotel we asked the question we've just asked you. It seemed that this train of thought was a revelation to them.

So it is all just a matter of allowing people to think from the outside in, understanding customer needs and organizing around them? Well, yes and no. You see it is not quite that simple. For people to deliver the great experiences they need to understand the organization's strategy. That strategy needs to explicitly state the role of customers and how the company plans to deliver on their needs. Consider the following questions:

- Does everybody know what your company's strategy is?
- Is that strategy centered on your customers?
- As you talk to people, are they inspired by your strategy?
- Do people support the processes, did they design them?
- Are they rewarded based on process and strategy or just on activities?
- Can your company elaborate on what Successful Customer Outcomes look and feel like?
- Do you train managers and analysts to be leaders?

The answers to these questions will provide you with great insight and help you to understand where the gaps are as you move into the Age of the Customer, and the next few chapters will help you develop ideas and plans to address the issues you are likely to find.

So we can now see that in the Age of the Customer, the customer is at the center of everything. This means that we will have to create and share an outside-in strategy that will allow us to organize around the customer. This strategy has to be communicated in ways that allow our people to buy in and understand how what they do supports it. Then, by using smart processes to enable our people to deliver Successful Customer Outcomes, we can change our organization to support those outcomes, resulting in increased revenue and profits. There is one final observation to share at this stage and that is around *leadership*. In order to inspire others and execute on strategies, organizations need to look to leaders not just managers in order to deliver SCOs. People love to be inspired by and motivated by good leaders. This is what we will consider in Chapter 5.

Case Study: Credit Where Credit's Due

Imagine you're running a credit card business. Turnover and profits are growing year after year, your staff are very satisfied (at industry leading levels in fact), and performance metrics are all looking great. Would you be happy? The management team of Capital One's UK business wasn't. They felt that the business wasn't working properly and set about finding out what was wrong.

Their analysis concentrated on how successful they were being in delivering what customers wanted. What they found was simple, striking and in real need of correction. This is the sort of conversation that the management might have listened in to:

Operator:	Welcome to Capital One, Mr. Everyman. My name is Jody, how can I help you?
Tom:	Hi. I'd like to pay off my balance today, please. Can you give me a settlement figure?
Operator:	I'm sorry, sir, but I can't give you that information over the phone.
Tom:	Oh. So how can I get that figure then?
Operator:	It will be in your next statement.
Tom:	So I have to wait until that arrives to pay you?
Operator:	Yes sir. Would you like to know when your next statement is due?
Tom:	I guess so.

Operator:	That will be in two weeks time.
Tom:	*Two weeks?*
Operator:	That's right, sir. Is there anything else I can help you with today?
Tom:	Well, no.
Operator:	Thank you for calling Capital One, Mr. Everyman. Goodbye.

Operational performance measures in the call center included two key components: call handling times and an assessment of whether customers were being given the right answers to queries. By these measures this was a successful call: three accurately answered questions in a short space of time. Clearly the wrong things were being measured, and this was masking the shortcomings of the processes that were supposed to be delivering solutions for customers.

The measurement regime was soon changed to concentrate on Successful Customer Outcomes. Management responsibilities for fixing system and process limitations were sorted out, and frontline staff were enabled to deliver what customers really wanted and not what the MI demanded. The lesson is clear – look beyond the numbers to understand what your business is really about.

"People that think logically are a nice contrast to the real world."
—Matt Biershbach

5. The Importance of People

In earlier chapters we have talked about the importance of understanding what customers want, aligning the organization to these objectives, and delivering consistently. Here we will concentrate on another element, one that is at least as important because it is one of the key enablers for making the changes necessary to become a fully SCO-oriented company.

The proper implementation of SCOs will be a major shift for most organizations. Experience tells us that step change is almost always preceded by great insight, an individual with a clear vision acting as a catalyst for revolution. In the spirit of going beyond best practice (the concept of *Next* Practice which we will cover in Chapter 7) let's look outside the commercial world for examples of such catalysts.

There have of course been many great leaders: Alexander the Great, Winston Churchill, Elizabeth I, Abe Lincoln, JFK and Nelson Mandela are just a few of the names that resonate. Columbus and Magellan brought us a new understanding of our world through their exploration, while great thinkers like Aristotle, Einstein, Newton and Galileo pushed the boundaries of knowledge. Society has also benefited from the work of Mother Teresa and Louis Pasteur.

There are many others. Think of the greatest human achievements, those things that we all acknowledge as new and earth shattering. There were people at the center making stuff happen, reforming rather than conforming, pushing against the tide of opinion, resisting the momentum of current belief. What do all these people have in common? They were Masters of Mindset. They knew how to link the new with the old and take people with them into a new way of doing things. Of course the "technologies" helped but these were largely developed as a consequence of insight – not as a means to it. The Masters of Mindset needed people to understand, become convicted and then implement their vision. Those great people helped to articulate a roadmap that we could trust and follow.

The greatest catalysts for change the world has ever known had three qualities that helped them achieve the conditions for great victories or momentous changes:

Belief that the accepted ways of doing things are no longer appropriate.

There have always been rebellious types, people who go against the flow, if only for the sake of being contrary. Here though, we are talking about constructive opposition to the majority view. For example, Churchill, during the rise of Hitler, springs to mind. His opposition meant being a lone voice in the wilderness, risking ridicule and isolation. He clearly believed that the accepted ways of doing things were no longer appropriate, and he took a stand that changed history. Such stands are also key to business change.

Conviction that a new way exists that better fits a new order.

To be constructive, a critical view needs to incorporate an alternative. This alternative may have been arrived at through scientific investigation, unexpected insight or a personal belief system. Whatever the route, the commitment to the new perspective matches the opposition to the prevailing view. The importance of creating viable options and choices is undeniable: "Let's go this way" has more going for it than "Don't go that way!"

Courage and tenacity in driving towards that endeavor.

Silent objection has its place. It can be a key ingredient in significant change, magnifying the impact of a small event, generating an unstoppable momentum in a short space of time. The abolition of slavery in the U.S. and the end of apartheid in South Africa were accelerated in the end by the willingness of many to accept a new view. But these changes needed a catalyst, a visible vocal representation of the alternative – a Lincoln, a Mandela. To reach the silent objectors or mass public opinion someone has to be brave enough to speak out and keep speaking out until the objective is reached.

In our quest to move into the Customer Age and the delivery of SCOs we should draw on the lessons from the past Masters of Mindset and develop these three characteristics as individuals, teams, organizations and communities. If history tells us anything it is that mastering mindsets can be enormously powerful in effecting major shifts in thought and deed. We can also be sure that some pretty important things would not have happened if everyone had just sat around waiting for someone else to start. You can ask yourself this question – how well formed are your convictions that "the way things are done around here" aren't right? The leaders we've talked about worked hard at questioning the conventional view and understanding its shortcomings. To be ill-informed is to be ill-prepared, so get to know enough about how and why things don't work for you if you want to demonstrate how different the new world could be.

How does this set of behaviors translate into the workplace when, perhaps, there aren't the scientific and social ideals to be pursued? Just because the business of doing business may not seem as glorious an endeavor as working for world peace, there's no reason to use lower standards. Organizations of all kinds are as likely to suffer from a herd mentality as society as a whole, so the challenges of changing belief and mindsets are the same. The second generation of the Masters of Mindset has many things in common with those mentioned above. As believers in their cause, they learn how to communicate their beliefs in such a way as to inspire others, and they are great leaders. The difference is that the second generation doesn't lead armies or countries – they lead organizations.

Organizations such as FedEx, Southwest Airlines, Go Fly, Virgin Group, Ryanair, Google and Apple are good examples of the results achieved by the new generation of mindset masters. An interesting commonality, besides the obvious one about focusing on Successful Customer Outcomes, is that all place a strong emphasis on people.

These business leaders realized very early on in their development that the happier their people were, the happier those people would make their customers, a correlation that seems to be borne out in our personal experience of traveling around the globe. Barbara Cassini, former CEO of the budget airline GO, wanted to make sure that her staff really bought in to the company's different values, and for her the best example of surveying and motivating staff came from Richer Sounds, the retail store in the USA. All of the new low cost airlines give credit to Southwest for developing the business model for them, but it is interesting that they have still not captured the magic created by the people skills of Southwest President Colleen Barrett in really making everyone feel part of the family.

Fred Smith of FedEx had in mind creating an organization that wanted to serve its customers right from the start, and over the years FedEx has institutionalized such actions and behaviors to the extent that everyone in the organization knows who the customer is and how what they do relates to serving customers. Over at Google, the whole idea of the Googleplex is to make employees happy so that they work harder to serve their customers, and judging by the share price, it is working pretty well! Apple meanwhile has certainly had its ups and downs but few could argue that, during the periods with the charismatic Steve Jobs at the helm, it has mainly been ups.

These second generation masters are consummate leaders. They tend not to work in the vein of the archetypal MBA, but instead focus on communication, shared vision and shared values to lead their people and their organizations. They have the power to make a real difference, and that is something that people want to aspire to.

Herb Kelleher, former CEO of Southwest Airlines, noticed one day that, despite all the efforts of everyone, it appeared that morale was dropping and harmony was being disrupted in the company. He sat back, talked to others, and then came to the realization that for many years the company's people were almost working as an army against a foe. He then realized that the morale and harmony issue was because they no longer had a common enemy, a cause to fight for. In response, Kelleher focused everyone's attention on key areas of competition. He urged them all to unite to take on the threats to their survival, just as army tribal leaders have done for generations.

The lesson here is that for organizations to be truly successful they need true leaders not just managers. Indeed all the leaders and organizations discussed are outperforming their peers by considerable margins. These leaders understand people and emotions and are not be afraid to bring emotion to work. They spend more time learning about communication and language than they will about numbers and spreadsheets. And finally they make their organizations into places where people like us want to work!

Case Study: Frustration in Hospitality

What SCO-inspired survival tips can we propose that may help the hotel industry to avoid customer frustration and deliver ever greater value to their guests? Let's start in a place that may be familiar to many of you.

Another Night Away

The hotel bar was in the quiet lull between afternoon meetings and pre-dinner drinks. Tom Everyman sat alone, browsing the menu for something both edible and claimable. A smartly dressed member of the hotel staff approached – it was the manager.

"Excuse me, sir. I hope you don't mind me asking, but I see you have a tag on your luggage, showing you're a Gold Card holder with another hotel chain. Have you considered registering for our card?"

Tom was happy to respond. "I don't actually spend enough nights with your hotels to make it worthwhile, I'm afraid. But that's very observant of you, and thanks for asking."

"Well sir, if you don't mind me making a note of your room number, I'll arrange for Head Office to match the level of membership you have on your current scheme."

The hotel manager took the number from Tom's key fob and left. Tom swapped the menu for a list of hotel locations. There would be no harm in trying out his new card, and it felt okay to be wanted."

In the UK, at least, it is common practice for supermarkets to accept the competition's coupons, so why don't hotels take a leaf out of their book? As any frequent traveler knows, once you have gained Gold or Platinum status with one chain it is very hard to justify using other hotels unless you have to. If the others want your business they will have to work harder to get it.

Many frequent travelers also have changing travel habits: one year you travel a lot, the next not so much, the year after it picks up again. How frustrating is it to get great service as a Platinum member during your middle, less traveled, year, only to find that as your travel picks up you are downgraded again. In effect, regular customers are obliged to reconsider where to take their business and are open to influence. Why then don't hotels consider "lifetime" programs, with qualification over a period of years? Past customers are more likely to be future customers if you have a good product, so treat them like you want them to keep coming back.

In fact there are many ways that loyalty schemes could extend their benefits for the people they are aimed at. Question: when are hotel guests not hotel guests? Well, when they're not staying at the hotel is the answer, certainly from the hotel's perspective. Is there any reason why that should be, though? The interaction is more than just staying the night. Much more could be done to entice regular customers to use a hotel's facilities, for meetings or a catch up on email and phone messages over coffee. Free drinks and Internet access would be a small price to pay for all of the additional business that would be encouraged. In recent years many hotels have made great strides with creative use of the "Executive Lounge" concept, but there is still some way to go before they truly get it nailed.

On the subject of Internet access, isn't it strange how the lower-cost hotels are increasingly providing free high speed connections, whereas the up-market brands in the same chains still assume that it is acceptable to charge large sums for the privilege? In today's world it is not just the business traveler that relies on such niceties as high speed Internet – even leisure travelers are looking for this sort of service (especially as more and more people switch to using the Internet to make telephone calls).

And why charge for breakfast when the coffee shop across the street offers a better deal. Not only is the coffee better, but the café is probably a wi-fi hotspot – more lost opportunities.

Surely the time has come for the up-market brands to realize that if they are to compete, this practice has to change. It is no longer acceptable to assume that people will pay a premium price for a hotel and then be expected to pay again when there are free or cheaper alternatives.

It is unfortunate that in the hospitality industry, with the volume of bookings made, things will go wrong sometimes. As customers, we actually do understand this, but it is the ability to resolve the problem speedily and to our satisfaction that will set the best providers apart. This is simply delivering on the promise, the promise that said we could have a room. If there is a problem then what we want to hear, at least, is that alternative accommodation will be organized locally and any additional costs will be met. Again, the place to look for inspiration is retailing – perhaps a variation on the guaranteed returns policy might be something to aspire to?

The final group of suggestions for improvement relate to getting suggestions for improvements! Have you ever seen one of those signs saying something like "as requested by our frequent guests" or "in response to customer demand?" Have you ever wondered who these helpful customers are? We have. A straw poll of regular travelers generated little evidence that this seasoned section of the hotel user market is tapped for feedback. Keeping in regular contact with your best customers is an absolute necessity for product innovation and customer retention. Perhaps management spends disproportionate amounts of time analyzing those guest questionnaires that are always left in rooms. They are mainly filled out by infrequent guests who had that one great experience and do it as a thank you. Most of the business guests we have spoken to say they can't be bothered. So perhaps the surveys are self-serving.

Compare this approach to that of top retailers, who frequently run events for their best customers, inviting them to previews, discount nights and other events. Customers are encouraged to keep coming back, and it's an opportunity to talk on a one-to-one basis with them while keeping an eye out for changing buying habits. It's also a great way to pick up market intelligence on their competitors from the people who really know – the competitors' customers!

This raises another critical factor for service improvement in hotels – pay more attention to the feedback from front desk staff and less from middle management. The managers are aware of only the small proportion of issues that occur in the process, whereas front desk staff see them all. In any situation the best source of pain points will be front line staff, and they will also usually have some good ideas on how to improve the situation, very often at little or no cost.

These examples are taken both from our own experiences and those of people we have traveled with and coached. The suggestions are not scientifically based but are the results of people looking from the outside in. In many of the instances where bad service occurred it was put right, rarely though by an employee working within the system, but by one who recognized the lifetime value of a customer and attached an importance to that value. Hopefully, if enlightened hotel chains take heed of at least some of the advice and ideas, then all of our future travel experiences might get a little bit better.

"These are not high-level academic questions for economists, they are questions that your company and you, personally, must answer."
—Peter Fingar, author of *Extreme Competition*

6. The Importance of Process

In some organizations, responsibility for processes ranks alongside accountability for stationery in the subtle hierarchy of jobs to aspire to. This isn't surprising considering that these same organizations see process management as an administrative activity – the unspoken belief being that the job involves looking after piles of paper covered in lines and boxes that purport to represent what goes on in the business.

An even greater reason to keep process management at arms length in some eyes is that PM lies in that murky area between IT and business – a no man's land into which no one valuing their career options would be foolish enough to go. Process maps can look suspiciously technical, part of the alchemy that converts a business need into a new system.

In recent times many organizations have had to initiate process-related programs to meet the requirements of regulators – Sarbanes-Oxley for example. Often driven by the Risk or Audit functions, the emphasis of these programs is on control and transparency. This is certainly necessary, given the underlying objectives, but it's hardly lighting the fires of staff or customers.

Process Management should be something that

gets businesses excited, for one reason: processes are what connect employees and customers. Processes are what your people do and they are what your customers experience. A company that does not recognize its processes and is not making them work for the customer and staff is basing its strategy on luck.

There are some basic considerations that all companies should take into account when putting in place PM disciplines.

1. PM is more than just technology

Most of what you will read about Process Management will be generated in one way or another by people and organizations with an interest in systems and software. When we hear about the pace with which the PM market is growing, it is the expenditure on applications and solutions that is generally being portrayed. It would be easy to believe therefore that PM is about technology, but there's much more to it than that – it's about touching raw nerve ends. No Process Management application can tell you what your processes are or what they should be, no more than a word processing application will tell what your weekly progress report should say.

Looking more widely, there are many opinions as to why so many systems implementations go awry, and there are no magic answers to this thorniest of topics. Technology is an enabler and can make the difference to the execution of processes at the level of quality and cost that is needed. Technology won't make the wrong processes right though. If you only start understanding how your business works when you start the definition and design stage of a major systems implementation then the chances of success are already limited. Automate what you know.

2. It's all about performance

It's often said that it is not possible to manage revenue, cost and service all at the same time. At least it's often said by those who don't process manage their organizations. PM gives you the capability to manage the three points of the performance triangle by bringing them together in customer-focused chains of related activities. In a customer-led world, pursuing cost reduction to the exclusion of all else is only putting off the inevitable.

Processes cut across functional silos, bringing disparate parts of a business together and bypassing hierarchies. We have all seen examples of individual teams and departments making great efforts to improve efficiency and effectiveness without properly considering the role they play in the delivery of what the customer wants. How useful is a sub-10 second relay runner who can't take the baton and pass it on? Streamlining processes improves results; streamlining teams and departments is just about saving money.

3. People and process are inseparable

Anyone taking the technology sales pitch for process management too literally could end up believing that taking people out of processes is a good thing. The opposite is true. The goal should be to get people and process working in harmony, where staff are enabled to do the important things and can concentrate on that. Too often people have to *contend* with processes, or lack of them, to make things happen.

This close inter-relationship between people and process points to another important factor – don't be tempted to embark on a process-related change program without engaging the users of the processes first. They are the ones who have the daily experience of what works and what doesn't. They will also tell you how far off the mark your understanding of a process is. Assume at your peril.

4. Build processes around SCOs

One of the first challenges facing a company moving towards Process Management is where to begin and end a process. As most activities in an organization are inter-related, there is an argument for defining an enormous process that starts with strategy definition and ends with reporting the year end numbers. Outside-in companies have the advantage of knowing what's important and recognizing that the focus is the customer. Your SCOs should set out clearly what you are trying to achieve, and your processes should be defined and managed to support them. This way you will get processes that begin and end with customers.

Clearly there are important activities in any company that aren't directly customer-serving (finance and planning are good examples). Processes should be defined and managed here too, but the relative priority is obvious. Organizations don't exist to plan, so the related processes are supporting processes and no more.

The relative importance of processes should also find its way into the performance management structures of the company. If employee remuneration is too heavily dependent on *support* process performance rather than *customer* process performance then the balance is probably not right.

5. Processes are the organization

Take a break from reading this book for a minute and consider how you would describe your company, and particularly your role in it, to a stranger. Spend a couple of minutes on it.

It's a little impractical for us to review what you have come up with, but our experience of having this discussion with people we come across is that many employ the pyramid to describe who's in charge and who does what. As we've seen this is a very old model (the customer is often bottom of the pile). A company's processes should define what it does, so why not try describing your company and your role in it in terms of processes – it might be educational.

While some people think that processes lie somewhere between the business and IT, a more positive perspective is that processes *unite* these parts of the organization. Processes provide a common language for describing what the business does, offering some common ground on which to co-operate in achieving those SCOs.

The study of processes is a big subject in its own right. What's the best method to get started? We would suggest using an established framework to understand where you are and where you need to go. For starters, you might want to try the free 8Omega framework at the non-profit Business Process Management Group (www.bpmg.org). Wherever you start, start somewhere.

"The empires of the future are the empires of the mind."
—Winston Churchill

7. Being As Good As the Rest Is Not Enough

There is one other principle to add to this mix, a differentiating factor that will in many cases make the difference between the leaders and followers (and failures). With all of the attention organizations are lavishing on their internal workings, it is not surprising that the urge to compare themselves with competitors arises. If you have gone to the trouble of measuring and understanding your processes, drivers of cost, and service levels why not find out how they compare with others?

The push toward measurement and judgment based on such measures is to be applauded. It has long been argued that you can't change what you can't see and of course you can't manage what you can't measure. What can be questioned though is how to put this analysis to best use and how to manage an organization based on the measures that have been put in place.

Benchmarking and best practice will be terms that many are familiar with. They come from the same angle – how are we doing in relation to other businesses and what can we learn from others to improve ourselves. Fair enough, but these ideas can be very limiting in the context of a truly customer-oriented enterprise.

Becoming an outside-in organization is all about enabling new ways of working and adapting to rapid change – either to respond to market changes or to allow fast entry into new areas of business. As we have said, too much emphasis has been placed on the quest for "cheaper, faster, better," an approach that can have only a limited scope in the area of corporate survival. The scope is limited because if all companies chase "cheaper, faster, better" and benchmark themselves against each other then there comes a point of diminishing return. More importantly, in any given market the chances are that a new entrant will come in and do things completely different and play by a different set of rules. Simply doing the same things cheaper, faster and better will not ensure that companies survive.

No one is suggesting that this approach will not bring great benefit though: most companies will find through process analysis that they can drive out costs, while improving the speed of delivery of products of services and improving the quality of their operations. This is only a basic improvement, stage one if you like.

In the same way, benchmarking and best practice will ensure that you are not letting your competitors get ahead of you in the market. Let's call this a stage 2 improvement.

Smart companies, though, will be aiming to try and make a stage 3 improvement. Stage 3 can be thought of as "Next Practice."

Next Practice is about taking best practice, in fact any ideas, and applying them in new and innovative ways that competitors have either not done or not thought of doing yet! The beauty of Next Practice is that the inspiration is all around; we do not have to invent anything in order to get started on our journey. The first step in Next Practice is to change the criteria for benchmarking and best practice.

Most companies, when looking at benchmarking, look at the best of their competitors and judge themselves against these companies. It certainly serves as a reasonable starting point and provides some targets to aim for, but are they really stretch targets? Who does the market leader benchmark against?

The same goes for best practice. Applying best practice in process terms will certainly allow you to improve, and in the eyes of the customer may even be the difference between remaining in business or totally disappearing, but again, what about the market leader?

Next Practice demands that in the first instance you look at the very best companies in your domain and try to apply their standards. For example if you are a small software development company you will tend to look at how the likes of Microsoft or IBM develop and market their software. The challenge is that most of your competitors (assuming that they even look outside their sector) will be doing the same – the result is hardly earth shattering. But what if you looked at others who have built their reputations on delivering high quality R&D products outside of the software development arena (pharmaceuticals, for instance) and copied them? What if you looked to brand-based companies such as Coca-Cola for your ideas on marketing; looked at someone like Amazon for your inspiration in building on-line shops for your products; considered McKinsey as your inspiration for providing service. These examples may not be the best ones, but we are sure you will agree that a software company that delivered product to the same quality as a pharmaceutical company, services to the standard of McKinsey, while being as smart at brand awareness as Coca-Cola and as easy to buy from as Amazon would cause more than a few ripples in their marketplace.

The world of commerce is filled with great examples of how to do things better, and more companies should look outside of their own industry. The companies that do, and then bring those practices into their own industry, will be seen as no less visionary than those who come up with truly new ways of doing things but at considerable cost.

Historically, the idea of Next Practice has not been easy to apply. Sure, the idea is there for all to see, but to actually implement the idea presents a great challenge. Without a clear understanding of how you currently do things and a detailed understanding of the assets available, such ideas have often been seen as nothing more than mere dreams in the boardroom. Process-based approaches to business have now changed all that. Using the maps and measurements that have all too often been used to simply automate existing processes, you can readily identify how you can apply best practice in your business. Companies that have truly embraced a process approach will find it much easier and quicker to take on Next Practice. If you want to know whether your organization is one of these then check off the following:

- Processes mapped.
- Strategy and vision incorporated in process thinking.
- People trained to be highly attuned to the concepts of change.

How did you do? Few get more than a couple of check marks.

Companies that have focused themselves on the customer, organized around that, and aligned their people appropriately have achieved most of what they need to be successful in the new world. But the leaders are doing something else too – they aren't just reacting quickly to change, they are anticipating it, and sometimes driving it themselves. To do this they have created working environments that generate forward leaps in innovation. When most organizations are consumed by reacting to crises, they are at a distinct advantage.

So this right-brain thinking takes the benefits of best practice (successful in the car industry, for instance, which was transformed by the widespread adoption of Japanese production techniques) and moves them on to a new level. The difference is that customers are looking for added value, and simply following the rest of the pack isn't going to work.

There will be some readers who will see that this may apply to other businesses but does not apply to them. Either because they see that it is too difficult, just another passing fad, or because they feel that no one else in their industry does it either.

Others will see that Next Practice is only just the beginning, for once you have applied the concept of Next Practice in your industry, then surely others will try to follow on the basis that you will now have set the benchmarking and best practice standards by which your competitors will want to judge themselves.

Whereas you will have seen that having applied Next Practice, by embedding good process management practices and a culture of change within your organization, you have only just started to raise the bar. For now you will be able to couple and uncouple processes and practices in new and innovative ways, ways that could cause great disruption in your chosen marketplace.

To be able to create mini-monopolies, be the sole provider in the space, and then move on as soon as the competition catches up is a powerful place to be. It is the companies that are able to cause such constant "disruption" in their markets that will emerge as the true market leaders.

Case Study: Changing the Face of Public Service

In many countries, the phrase public service is considered something of an anachronism. At all levels of government and government-led services, customers perceive that overall they get a raw deal when compared to the levels of service they now regularly expect from privately held organizations. This case study explores how Customer Age thinking and the concepts of Successful Customer Outcomes and Next Practice are helping to change that perception and lead to increased efficiency in public services around the globe.

We first need to remember that in a democracy, government is of the people, by the people, with the will of the people. As governments increasingly raise taxes and start to play a more active role in the everyday lives of people there is a real risk that, if they do not focus on their customer and what the customer wants, they might lose that will. So for government departments at all levels there needs to be clarity on who the customer is and what they want. In this they are no different from a private enterprise. Customers do not care about your internal bureaucracy or your policies and procedures, but they do care about being able to access your services in an efficient manner and know that they are being cared for.

Nobody is suggesting for one moment that you can please everybody. But if those that you are not pleasing are displeased because of poor service or overly complicated procedures and policies, then in most cases, they have good cause to complain. Indeed, employees (civil servants) in the public sector would do well to remember that it is their tax money that is being potentially wasted too!

Many people might feel that government and public sector is a special case and that the same rules cannot apply. To a small extent this may be right, but in the majority of cases fresh thinking can still lead to increased service and efficiency.

Take the case of a police force. While recently working with a regional police department the point was raised that they are a very different business, unlike anything in the private sector. This is typical of the inside-out thinking that tends to occur in public service. It we look at it from the outside in, the police force could be considered rather like an insurance company. The parallel is quite a simple one. With insurance we pay a monthly or annual premium to a company on the promise that if something goes wrong we can contact them and they will sort it out – cars, home, or life. So in the case of the police, we pay taxes each month (our premium) so that if something goes wrong we can contact them and they will send someone to help us. Surely this is the same, from the customer point of view, as the insurance scenario. The same can be said of the fire and ambulance services. Why then can such services not look at what insurance companies are doing in order to improve service and responsiveness?

As a side issue, in another discussion with a different police service the issue of customer became apparent in a different way. In this force they felt that the way they had been organized was to ensure that they provided the best service to their customer, it was just that in their case they saw the criminal as the customer, not the victim! So when identifying your customer you do need to be clear on your purpose in order that you are serving the right customers.

The example of the emergency services given here is a good example of how Next Practice can be applied in the public service, and how in looking for new and innovative ways to improve service and increase efficiency the public sector can benefit from looking at how the very best people are handling that situation, regardless of geography or industry sector.

The parallels do not end there though. Those familiar with the Beatles may recall a track on Sergeant Pepper's Lonely Hearts Club Band (an oldie but a goodie) called "A Day in the Life" which mentions "4,000 holes in Blackburn, Lancashire." The song relates John Lennon's curiosity at how many holes it would take to fill the Albert Hall (a particularly large musical venue in central London) and indeed why there were so many holes? Well clearly at that time he had never visited Chicago as they have enough holes to fill the Grand Canyon!

The story of how the Chicago Works Department transformed a moribund public service (fixing said potholes), which typically took six to eight weeks, involved up to thirty people, and on average cost an incredible $42,000 USD, is now becoming legend in

Process Management parlance.

The quantum leap here with Next Practice and Successful Customer Outcomes drew its inspiration from Expedia. Daniel Pink (A Whole New Mind) would be proud of the right brain thinking which imported Expedia's scheduling 'idea' to transform the service: citizens were given the ability to identify the problem, chose a suitable repair, and select a convenient date for the work via a two screen web based system. Problem fixed. Now on average a repair takes four days, five people and $2,000 USD. That still seems a lot (especially for tax payers) for filling a hole but boy is it giant step in the right direction!

Of course we can extend this thinking even further into many walks of public service. Where would you start your Next Practice endeavors?

"Man's mind, once stretched by a new idea, never regains its original dimensions."
—Oliver Wendell Holmes, Jr.

8. Ten Reasons Why SCOs Will Never Take Off in Your Organization!

Now this may seem an ill-advised chapter, given what we're trying to do here but there's a good reason for including this chapter. We should remember that organizations have defined themselves by *function* for many years. Managers and executives have spent a long time, both in on-the-job training and through management training centers, learning how to become better specialists.

The very idea that a few so-called "gurus" could suggest that they should turn their organizations outside-in and put the customer at the center of everything seems more than a little amusing to them. To many these gurus should spend more time in the "real" world, understanding what goes on, instead of causing problems by converting some of their middle and senior managers to a new way of thinking.

It is this apparent lack of understanding of the people issues that may ultimately stall any momentum towards a better way of working. It is not sufficient to talk to the generic "Company," "Customer" or "Organization," if the "Me" factor is not addressed. This may seem rather strange for an approach which talks of empowering people and promises greater freedom.

But there are questions that people will always have when faced with change: "Why should I engage with this? We might be able to save the company money, but what will I get out of it? Will it make my life easier? What about my chances of a salary raise or maybe a promotion?" If we want to get people to do something, then in addition to appealing to the corporate issues we need to address the personal ones too. Companies and markets are after all just collections of individual people.

As we look at the ten reasons why Successful Customer Outcomes won't take off in your organization, we will see the importance of understanding and then addressing the key obstacles to effecting major change in organizations. Listen to the "voice of resistance" below.

Reason 1: Promoting Professional Change.

"You are suggesting that we promote the idea that we have to move from where we are, to some greener pasture elsewhere. The thing is, we actually quite like being where we are, thank you! We do not see a need for our company to move with all these new fangled ideas. We have been in business since way before you were born and have always served our customers well. The idea that we might not have customers later is just too preposterous for words.

Besides, there is already too much change in society and our customers and staff just won't stand for any more. It is our duty to stand firm and be an organization that people can depend on."

Reason 2: Removing Islands of Information and Silo Thinking

"Applying Successful Customer Outcomes will help to eliminate islands of information and silo thinking from within organizations. These things may well be a problem in someone else's organization, but they are not a problem here. I meet regularly with my peers and can get access to any information I require from them. Sure, some of it might be a little out of date or difficult to track down, but we have people who can sort that out and it does not really add to our costs.

As for silo thinking, we have been all through that debate many times. We cannot see any purpose in giving people visibility outside the areas they are working in. We take great pride that our engineers provide the best components, and our marketers know how to market our products as well as anyone."

Reason 3: The Importance of Communication

"Promoting communication is all very well if you want to do that. In this organization we have management and it is their job to communicate what is needed, to the people that need to know. And to be honest we probably already have more communication than we need. It is far easier to manage our people if we only drip feed the information to them. They are probably not capable of dealing with much more anyway."

Reason 4: Focusing on Managing by Measurement

"We already have all the measures we need – we don't need any more. What you don't understand is that measures mean accountability, and I quite like the fact that I can fudge the numbers in the current system. The idea of greater accountability fills me with dread and the fact that they might all be linked up in a cohesive manner will sound great to the bosses, but down here we don't want that.

In any case, I am not aware of anyone who has found themselves earning more money or getting promotion as a direct result of managing more measures, especially in areas like quality."

Reason 5: Moving Away From a Command & Control Structure

"To do this properly we would have to consider moving away from a command and control structure, which makes it simply unworkable in our organization. Our very strength and indeed that of our competitors lies in organizational structure. We have spent years evolving and refreshing it, and it is the very heart of our company. People rely on it to know their status within the organization and what is expected in their role. It is also vital in establishing pay grades, salary structures, benefits and bonuses – such things would just not work in a flatter organization."

Reason 6: It's Not All About Technology

"Being really customer-oriented is not all about technology. However, we have had numerous presentations from many IT vendors who say just the opposite. In fact, we like the idea of a pure technology solution. As an IT function we know how to handle such projects and have the knowledge and capabilities, built up over many years, to implement them. The last thing we need is a concept that requires us to further engage with the business. The idea that technology is just an enabler for business is not something we believe round here."

Reason 7: It's Not Rocket Science

"We have a highly experienced executive team and numerous MBAs within our senior and middle management; these people know how to go looking for solutions. We have invested in them, to enable them to seek out these solutions and many of them could deal with rocket science. If it were that straightforward we could just train our existing people and empower them to make the changes we need. No, it can't be that simple or straightforward."

Reason 8: Investment in Training and Education

"This is going to need a lot of investment in training and education. Here in our company we can't be spending money training people on this. If we do that they will all want training. Besides if everyone was trained in it, they would all be asking questions all the time and we can't have that. Management won't know the answers, which would lead to anarchy. We won't be able to spare the time of the management team in education, they are too important for that."

Reason 9: Promoting Common Sense

"Successful Customer Outcomes are all about common sense, understanding what you have, what you need, and developing a plan to help you get there. All sounds fine in theory. However, if business was just about common sense then everyone would be doing it, wouldn't they? We have worked very hard to create something very special, and complexity just adds to our competitive advantage. Simplicity is all very well, but it's easy for others to replicate so what's the point?"

Reason 10: It's a Boardroom Issue

"There's just not enough time to consider any more issues of this size. Perhaps you don't understand, but we have a very full agenda here in the executive suite. We are trying to figure out strategies for growth and corporate direction. We don't have time to waste on new-fangled ideas that have yet to be proven. We pay people an awful lot of money to look at these sorts of things – if anything good emerges, we will soon hear about it from them.

Besides it's all about customers and people and processes. We focus on bigger things up here, real numbers and real strategies. I can't imagine anyone improving their bottom line significantly by fiddling about with that sort of stuff."

* * *

Okay, so this is a little tongue in cheek. But it serves to highlight the real issues faced by anyone looking to make change happen in organizations of any kind. The challenge we all face is how to ensure that our colleagues and companies understand that these are the real problems they face. SCOs won't solve all the problems of the world, but then what new management paradigm can? A few of the quotes warrant further examination, so we'll explore them a little.

Reason Two would be fairly typical of an engineering company (especially one which has adopted an improvement methodology like Six Sigma). We see that engineers build great components, but if they are not what the market wants then, regardless of how good the Marketing team is, people won't buy them and we are just wasting money again. It's so much easier to remove the silos and have the teams engage much earlier in the process and continue to do so throughout.

In Reason Three we took the example of the UK emergency services, all three of which (Fire, Police and Ambulance) while managed separately, spend a significant amount of their time working together. However, when the Countess of Wessex needed to get to hospital urgently for the birth of her baby, it was a policeman that arrived and not an ambulance. It turns out that everyone thought someone else was sorting the ambulance and so a well thought out plan fails in execution, due to the lack of communication. Luckily enough for all concerned, this potentially life threatening situation had a happy ending.

In our fourth example I had in mind the positive side of Six Sigma and companies like General Electric and Motorola. In these companies significant amounts of executive and management pay are directly linked to their achieving the requisite measures set by the company.

The seventh example, if you did not already guess, was Microsoft. In the early days they were just a couple of young people who saw an opportunity, and with a couple of quick moves created the beginning of a fairly successful company. Of note though is that, while many see Microsoft as a software or technology company, the key to Microsoft's strength lies not with the "Rocket Scientists" in their labs, but with their smart use of marketing. In many ways Microsoft is a marketing company that just so happens happens to deliver software.

The basis of Reason Eight was British American Tobacco. They attribute most of their success in implementing major change to the inclusive training programs they have put in place. When rolling out Process Management initiatives, the company took a great deal of time and trouble to put in place a training and education program. This has enabled managers, process engineers and line managers to all learn the same approaches, tools and techniques. This has resulted in extraordinary buy-in from the business.

There was no specific example behind Reason Ten. However, if we take the sum of all the previous examples, as well as a growing number of case studies, it is simply not possible to ignore the business benefits. However, the language used in the case studies may not yet be right for the boardroom. Indeed, the media too may be inappropriate. Perhaps when such stories are regularly carried in publications such as the *Harvard Business Review*, as was the case with stories such as GE and Motorola years ago, then we can hope to win the hearts and minds of the boardroom.

It is not all doom and gloom, but a lot of work is needed. Hopefully you will be reading this with an open mind and will take on board the problems discussed. For only by understanding the real motivations of our companies, our staff and our customers can we possibly begin to make the changes that are so badly needed.

"If you know the enemy and know yourself you need not fear the results of a hundred battles."
—Sun Tzu

9. More Than Words

You may by now have formed a view of what your organization needs to do to fully embrace the ideas behind Successful Customer Outcomes. What is more difficult is deciding where and when to start. So often the timing of major change is driven by impending problems. Of course, by then it may already be too late. The actions may simply slow down and prolong an agonizing downward slide. The worst thing of all is that, as a result, others may conclude that making the necessary changes won't make a difference.

In marketing, it is the company that has the vision and strength to continue to pour money into marketing during an economic downturn that truly cashes in when the market takes an upturn. These companies recognize that a) they can very often buy their marketing at significantly reduced cost, and b) they get much greater exposure as there tend to be fewer advertisers to compete with, and so they enjoy far greater public awareness, leading to greater sales when buyers return to the market.

In the case of change programs, the opposite is true. Companies that are constantly striving to improve themselves, while currently seeming strong already, win out in the long term. Such companies are always moving the barriers and making it harder for others to compete with them. On the other hand, companies that wait until they have serious problems before undergoing such change will more often than not run out of either time or money before the positive effects can truly kick in.

An example of this in the UK would be Marconi, the former electronics and defense giant. The company had for years been seen as a stalwart British company; no one could ever have imagined it going under. But, sure enough, after a couple of wrong moves, the company was in trouble. Had the company made changes faster, recognizing what needed to be done while it was still strong enough to act, it may well have survived. To be accurate, many would say that the company is still alive and continuing to do business, but the shareholders lost most of their money in the refinancing, and most of the staff lost their jobs.

Now it would be foolish to suggest that companies in trouble can't successfully undertake change and survive. But, as in the case of Marconi, the cuts and changes have to be far more dramatic than they might otherwise be, and while such companies might survive, very few attain the heights from which they will have fallen.

So you may be reading this and thinking that it does not apply to you or your company. That would be a grave mistake. The last twenty years have shown that all companies, large or small, new or long established, are vulnerable to new competitors and, of course, to the new world economy. Nothing is the same now, and nothing will remain the same in the next 5 or 10 years. All companies need to have a clear idea of what their value chains are and how their business processes operate and are managed. Without such knowledge, it is likely to prove impossible to respond to external changes and to make internal changes quickly enough to work out how to reduce cost without reducing capability, and thus to satisfy regulators that you actually understand how your business operates!

The next question to answer is how quickly you can introduce the new order to your organization: through evolution or revolution? There is no doubt that the pace of change in society as a whole is relentless. This means we have to strive to improve the ways in which we operate ever faster too. But what approach should we take to improvement? Continuous process improvement as suggested by the Total Quality Management approaches of old, step change improvements or the Big Bang approach?

This is the question nagging at the minds of many and it all boils down to two points. First, the level of disruption you or your market can take and, second, what your perspective is. As we shall see, strong corporate performance in the future is likely to be based on your ability to manage all three approaches to improvement, at the same time, both inside and outside your organization.

The pace at which we can manage change will vary according to company culture, people and markets. The challenge will be in understanding these factors and being able to apply such understanding in the smartest way possible.

At a recent conference there was a heated debate between two delegates over the difference between Big Bang and Step Change. After a long discussion it turned out that the two were in violent agreement – it was just that they were talking about completely different things! One was using Big Bang in the context of a project causing a switch from process A to process B at a specific point in time, whereas the other was referring to Big Bang as something that completely changed a market, e.g., caused massive disruption in the way Amazon did when creating a whole new way of buying books via the web.

So the first thing we need to establish when seeking to make change, is whether we are looking at it from a market, company or project perspective. In all cases we still will make use of the three levels of change – incremental, step and Big Bang. This differentiation is especially important in communicating change. Management will need to be clear when communicating such changes, as this context will have a major bearing on the receptiveness of the audience. As you might expect, people will be thrilled by the benefits that might come about by Big Bang, especially if it affects others and not them! Those same people are also more likely to prefer the idea of incremental change if it involves major changes to the way they work.

Whether it is a word that people like to see or not, disruption is the key differentiator between the three levels of change. Quite simply, incremental change implies minimal disruption, step change implies some disruption, and Big Bang implies major disruption.

The levels and benefits of disruption that you are looking for will depend largely on your perspective. When it comes to your markets, the more disruption you can cause your competitors then the more you can gain from your markets. Smart companies will be constantly looking at ways to apply disruptive solutions and make it as near impossible as they can for competitors to catch up with them. At the same time, if your perspective is inward, internal disruption will be minimized to ensure that you allow any changes to bed down before moving on.

When looking at your customers there is a fine line to be drawn between disruptive changes that they might appreciate, things that make it easier for them to buy or get service from you, and those that take them into areas that they are not comfortable with yet, e.g., switching everyone to online or telephone banking and doing away with branches.

It goes without saying that in all aspects of business incremental change is simply a necessity of life. It is not good enough to keep doing the same things. We have to do what we do ever better, and we have to deliver better products and services to our markets and customers. It should be taken as read that the culture in modern organizations should be adapted for such change.

However in reality even such minor change seems to cause disproportionate levels of disruption. This is probably due to ineffective communication on the part of management. Truly embedding incremental change as part of a culture means providing people with shared vision, involvement and communication.

Of course from a project perspective what might be seen by a company as incremental may, in fact, be seen as a major step change to the staff directly associated with it, and so when planning a project roll out consider whether greater emphasis in the training needs to be placed on gaining commitment from the staff involved.

The primary factor in managing change is people. Whatever your organization you will only be able to comfortably handle incremental change if you don't take into account people issues. In our lives today we all have to deal with too much change, and for many of us the thought of willingly bringing on more change fills us with dread. So in order to be able to manage step or Big Bang changes we need to invest in people. This investment in people is not merely providing them with communication and training in new methods, approaches and processes – although more effort in this area would certainly make it somewhat easier for people to deal with change at work.

Instead, it is more a case of working to develop people's receptiveness to change in all aspects of their lives. Employers who focus on "training for life" and helping their staff learn the skills to deal with change in their everyday lives would find those same staff far more willing to co-operate with change in their work organizations. In fact, we would go as far as to suggest that staff trained to understand and deal with change in their lives outside work would be far more likely to become proactive in changing aspects of their work in order to aid productivity.

However, as we have seen it is not just your staff you need to think of when dealing with the people issues: you also have to think about your market too. Whatever your field of business, the fact is that your end market will be made up of people. In assessing how much change your market can deal with, you will need to think about the people that make up your market and how willing they might be to adapt. There is no point in making a Big Bang change centered on technology if your target market is made up of older people, as for the most part, they are more than a little wary of all things technological. Witness the fact that until recently, most VCRs were being programmed by children for their parents!

So the real key in managing pace is to ensure that you, as opposed to your competitors, understand how receptive to change your people and markets are. Indeed, proactive companies will be those that actively seek to help those people and thus truly embed the change culture in their companies and markets. For that is what it is really about: changing the culture of a company or market to ensure that it is receptive to change. The more receptive it is then the faster and bigger the changes you can make.

Companies that are able to embed such culture will surely be the big winners in the months and years ahead.

"When we got into office, the thing that surprised me most was to find that things were just as bad as we'd been saying they were."
—John F. Kennedy

10. A Call to Action

We hope that have made the case for the changes that are coming and for the need for everyone to play their part in making the most of the opportunities (and, yes, they *are* opportunities) that will come with those changes.

We have highlighted some of the changes that are already taking place and showcased those people and organizations that are working hard to shape and make the most of the Age of the Customer. We have also pointed out examples of businesses that have not been able to respond to change and have fallen by the wayside.

Our examination of the management structures and priorities that dominate the world of organized activity has revealed many of the inadequacies for successfully conducting business the Age of the Customer. Hopefully, through our examination, the roots of these structures are a little clearer, as are the reasons for fundamental change.

Successful Customer Outcomes will have a major role in any organization's transition into the Age of the Customer, requiring as they do an overhaul of strategy and priority throughout the company. The extent to which you and your organization properly grasp this principle and make it work in practice will determine your success. If you can understand the importance of Moments of Truth and the impact they have on customer perception, you will be making important steps forward.

The following table summarizes some of our Case Studies in terms of the issues faced and the innovative SCO-oriented approaches taken:

Company	Problem	Approach
Otis Elevators	Cutting elevator waiting times in increasingly crowded office blocks	Brought in scheduling ideas from Japanese railway
easyJet	Cutting the cost of operation without reducing service offered	Sickness bags doubling as sponsored photo development packaging
Chicago Works	Hugely expensive and inefficient road repair service	Implemented Expedia-like book it yourself processes for residents
Capital One	Numbers good but company "feel" wrong	Overhauled measurement system to focus on customer

Figure 1. SCOs require both internal and external capabilities

People, and particularly leaders, have an enormous part to play in delivering organizations into the Customer Age. Masters of Mindset have long played a key role in times of massive change, and now is no different. People need great processes if they are to be able to do the right things for customers. Processes can also be the great integrator in today's fragmented businesses, allowing everyone in the company to work together in the combined objectives of raising company performance and customer satisfaction.

To learn from the best in your industry is the minimum requirement for success. The ability to take the leap beyond convention and current practice, into Next Practice, is what will create the winners. Some organizations are doing it already, so there is no time to waste.

There is no doubt that there will be obstacles to embracing the Age of the Customer, but attitude and action will be powerful weapons in the battle for progress. Understanding sources of opposition and reasons for wrong thinking will be a necessary part of your efforts to move your organization on to the next level.

We have one final request: don't wait for others to act first. There has been too much failure and missed opportunity in history to make this a good approach. We humans are not natural embracers of change. With some honorable (and some masochistic) exceptions we tend to favor the continuation of the norm. We may be happy to introduce change to ourselves, but we don't react well when others do it to us. Uncertainty is often the reason for this resistance, so any leader has to be prepared for rejection and antipathy over a period of time. Uncertainty is temporary, though, if you work hard enough. Stick with the SCO message and the obstacles will become smaller.

In the same way as you should understand why today's ways don't work, it's important to be very clear about how Successful Customer Outcomes will benefit you and the business you are part of. Hopefully this book has helped. Prove the benefits (to yourself as well as to others) by making a difference in any way you can. Mother Teresa changed the lives of many people in Calcutta by first changing the life of one person, then another. Apply the principles in a way that your colleagues will understand and the confidence that starts to flow will be catching.

Above all don't forget that you are a customer too. As an individual you may well be doing things now that you would never have imagined only a short time ago: making calls over the Internet; carrying 5000 songs (or your inbox for that matter) in your pocket; accepting the benefits of drinking bacteria from a plastic bottle. We all accept massive change in our lives and yet draw back from being the source of it ourselves. By taking an outside-in perspective we can all become embracers of change and deliverers of Successful Customer Outcomes. In the Customer Age there can be lots of winners: make sure you are one of them.

About the Authors

Steve Towers is the co-founder and CEO of the non-profit Business Process Management Group, a global business club exchanging ideas and best practice in BPM and change management. BPMG.org has over 19,000 members across all continents. Steve is one of the most tireless leaders in the field of business process management. While there are lots of technical folks and vested interests in the field, Steve's leadership rises above the crowd. Steve has traveled the world spreading the BPM message to business leaders and front-line workers, alike.

Mark McGregor is Director and Chief Coach of the BPM Group, a non-profit organization dedicated to furthering the aims and objectives of individuals and organisations in the Business Process Management field. Described by Gartner Group as a BPM Guru and by IQPC as a Master of Mindset, McGregor has contributed to many of the leading books on process and performance improvement. Learn more about Mark at his web site: www.markmcgregor.com

Your Complete BPM Library
Innovation at the Intersection of Business and Technology
www.mkpress.com

——The Landmark Book on BPM——
Business Process Management: The Third Wave
——New——

Extreme Competition, Peter Fingar
The World is Flat?, Aronica and Ramdoo
The Power of Process, Kiran Garimella
The Hyper-Competitive Business, Terry Schurter
More For Less, Andrew Spanyi

— www.mpress.com —